THEN & NOW

PHOENIXVILLE

An aerial view shows the Phoenix Steel Corporation as it appeared in the 1940s. With the plant in full operation, smoke billows from the many smokestacks. The vast network of buildings stretches from the Schuylkill River in the east to beyond the Gay Street Bridge in the west. With the exception of the foundry building, seen at the upper left, almost nothing remains of the once-mighty Phoenix Steel.

THEN & NOW

PHOENIXVILLE

Vincent Martino Jr.

ARCADIA PUBLISHING

ISBN 978-0-7385-3856-3

Published by Arcadia Publishing
Charleston, South Carolina

Printed in the United States of America

Library of Congress Catalog Card Number: 2005925673

For all general information contact Arcadia Publishing at:
Telephone 843-853-2070
Fax 843-853-0044
E-mail sales@arcadiapublishing.com
For customer service and orders:
Toll-Free 1-888-313-2665

Visit us on the Internet at www.arcadiapublishing.com

This auction house is seen in a late 1930s photograph. Located on Route 23, just west of the Route 113 intersection, this area was known as Toonerville. As indicated on the signs, auctions were held on Tuesday and Saturday evenings. Perhaps the most interesting aspect of this image is the decommissioned trolley car that was being used as a snack bar. Signs on the building and car tout Red Man Chewing Tobacco, Philip Morris Cigarettes, Burdan's Ice Cream, and nickel hotdogs. Today, nothing remains of the bucolic auction house or trolley car. The general vicinity is now home to a producer of building materials.

CONTENTS

The Pennsylvania Railroad station is seen in this photograph from 1912. It was located on Vanderslice Street, just west of the Gay Street Bridge. This was one of the few train stations that served the Phoenixville community for decades before the need for passenger rail service began to dwindle. Despite vehement protests, the shuttered station was torn down in the late 1980s. Today, the site is an overgrown lot, with only some steps and a partial foundation to indicate that the train station was ever there.

Introduction

As Phoenixville settles into the 21st century, the town marks more than 150 years since its incorporation. The community finds itself in the midst of a renaissance, a cultural, commercial, artistic, and demographic rebirth. The community is developing as a regional destination for working, living, and recreation, and great strides have been made in the residential, retail, and commercial sectors.

Arguably, change goes hand in hand with progress. Change is inevitable and sometimes regrettable, but one must embrace it or be overcome by it. Even those who have lived in Phoenixville for less than 10 years will remember many vanished structures and altered landscapes. The demolition of buildings in the name of progress has been rapid during the last decade. Fields once cultivated for crops are now excavated for housing. One can only imagine the types of changes witnessed by Phoenixville's older lifelong residents. As the famous proverb goes, "If there is one constant, it is change."

However, each person may adopt a different attitude in regard to change. When one person lauds the efforts of a developer, another may decry the wanton destruction of a community landmark. Fortunately, the power of memory can overcome the initial distress. Complementing these memories of the past are the photographs taken by Phoenixville's residents over the years. These images represent a window into the past. The evocative nature of an old photograph can transport anyone to any place at any time. Those who long for the "good old days" and those who crave nostalgia can be satisfied in this regard.

Phoenixville is a town so small that one can walk at a leisurely pace from end to end in a matter of hours. Yet despite its size, it is a town rich in history. Much of that history was wrought through the town's contiguity to Valley Forge and proximity to Philadelphia, but so much more originated in itself. Initially, the steel mill put Phoenixville on the map. At its height, the Phoenix Steel Corporation spanned practically the entire length of town, employed many of the community's residents, supported businesses of every type, and lent itself to the development of much-needed infrastructure. The steel mill, in its varying degrees of operation, has left an indelible mark on the town it called home.

Although Phoenix Steel once boasted scores of buildings around town, almost all have been demolished in the name of progress. These days, all that remains of the industrial behemoth are three structures: the foundry building on north Main Street, the superintendent's building on east Bridge Street, and the pump house, which sits on a barren tract of land just north of French Creek. For those who are new to Phoenixville, it is almost unfathomable to think of what little remains of an entity that the entire town was built around.

Although progress most certainly comes with a price, so does preservation. It is desirable for the purists among us to see an old building adapted for reuse. However, sometimes the cost of retrofitting an old building can be prohibitive. When developers examine opportunities for adaptive reuse, they must maintain practicality and remember the bottom line. But the sentimental viewpoint always favors preservation. Phoenixville is fortunate in that a vast majority of its original buildings have been preserved and are still in use.

Many people arrive in Phoenixville as visionaries, seeing the potential that exists in, for example, an old Victorian home. Others arrive out of opportunity or necessity. In any event, they will all make their mark in some way on the quilted fabric that is Phoenixville.

Now, take a journey back in time. Visit the many structures that remain virtually unchanged, including some that still serve their original intended use. Examine with hope and admiration the many buildings that have been creatively adapted for reuse. Be mesmerized by the changing landscapes that gradually incorporate small changes to create a cohesive result. And revisit or be introduced to a multitude of places that now exist only in our hearts and minds. As you embark, bear in mind that, in the current photographs, every effort was made to capture the same perspective shown in the older image. In some instances, new trees or buildings may obscure the modern camera's view, but the photograph reflects the subject in the most pure form possible.

The Phoenixville Memorial Works is seen in a 1930s photograph. Located on Nutt Road just west of Whitehorse Road, the business is still in operation today. Although original elements of the old barn still exist, a new addition to the front of the structure has made the façade almost unrecognizable today. Additionally, several mature trees obscure this enterprise, which sits right along busy Route 23. The old house at the right remains, albeit in a commercial capacity, but the rural character of this area is gone. (Historic image courtesy of Mrs. S. Martin Hamman.)

Chapter 1
STILL THE SAME

Constructed in 1838–1839, the 1,931-foot Black Rock Tunnel is seen in this early 20th century photograph. Several people, presumably railway workers and their children, are standing near the northern entrance to the tunnel. A small structure was used to shelter the workers while they performed the around-the-clock, year-round work that kept the trains moving safely through the tunnel. Although the tunnel is still in use today, the work originally performed by these workers is now automated. As a result, the small structure to the right became obsolete and was demolished long ago.

A 1910 photograph shows Nutt Road from the Manavon Street intersection. All of these homes are still in place, although many have been subdivided into multi-family dwellings. Nutt Road also constitutes busy Route 23 and is a major thoroughfare in the area. The serene nature of this historic image is no longer indicative of this heavily traveled road.

St. Mary's Catholic Church is seen in a photograph from 1910. The church is located on Dayton Street between St. Mary's and Emmett Streets. The church still serves a diverse group of Catholics and is one of four Catholic churches in Phoenixville. The dome has been removed from the church, but otherwise it exists much the same now as it did then.

A 1907 photograph shows St. Ann's Catholic Church and rectory at the corner of Main Street and Third Avenue. The construction of this church was made possible by a donation from the Byrne family. The church looks much the same today as it did then, although the bell tower has been enclosed. The small church in the background was a Hungarian church located on Third Avenue at Buttonwood Street. Today, that building is a private residence.

St. John's Reformed Church was constructed in the 19th century. Shown here in an image from 1912, the church has been remarkably well preserved in its original form. It still serves a diverse group of worshippers at its location on Gay Street between First and Second Avenues.

A photograph from 1915 shows the band shell located in Reeves Park, facing Main Street. Built at the beginning of the 20th century, the band shell has been the centerpiece of the park for decades and has played host to a variety of acts. As is evident in the current photograph, the potted palms, ornate statue, beveled-edge wood benches, and undeveloped fields have been lost to time and progress. Today, the park is home to a playground and a ball field and is host to various community events.

This is the Phoenixville Public Library as it appeared in 1905 and 2005. Although a century has passed, the library's main building appears much as it did when it was built in 1901 using grant money from wealthy tycoon Andrew Carnegie. Although the rooftop dome was removed long ago, the library looks much the same today as it did then. A 1987 renovation and addition updated the library and increased its capacity. It continues to serve the community at the corner of Main Street and Second Avenue.

Two groups of police officers are seen standing on the Second Avenue side of the library, which is located on Main Street. Pictured in 1905, unidentified officers wield nightsticks adorned with tassels. A century later, the camera captured four current members of the Phoenixville Police Department. From left to right are Officer Jose Sousa, Officer David Boyer, Sgt. Thomas Sjostrom, and Officer Patrick Mark. Interestingly, the older image clearly shows bars on the library's basement windows. Due to fire codes and the advent of elaborate alarm systems, these are no longer necessary.

The Valley Forge Army Hospital's post movie theater is pictured in the early 1950s. The original Valley Forge Army Hospital was located on Charlestown Road and bordered by Coldstream Road and Township Line Road. As military downsizing initiatives gained steam in the 1970s, the hospital was permanently closed. Today, the property functions as the Valley Forge Christian College. Although many of the original buildings have been preserved and adapted for reuse, the theater has been closed and sits in a state of disrepair.

The building shown here served the Valley Forge Army Hospital in an administrative capacity for decades. Today, it is one of the most prominent buildings on the campus of the Valley Forge Christian College. Despite the growth and progress experienced by the school during the past two decades, the building still looks much like it did in the photograph from the early 1950s. This grand building can be seen from the Charlestown Road entrance to the campus.

The post office is seen in this 1939 view. Located on Gay Street at Church Street, this facility was built to accommodate the needs of Phoenixville's fast-growing community. Although the building has received several interior modifications over the years, the exterior remains much the same today, save for the addition of an access ramp. Years ago, the acquisition of some neighboring homes allowed the post office to expand and create additional parking at the site.

The Phoenixville Area High School was built in 1956. Located at the corner of Gay Street and City Line Avenue, the school has undergone a massive renovation aimed at accommodating a growing population and new demands in education. Although the façade has not changed significantly since this photograph was taken in 1958, the landscaping has become more elaborate and some small superficial modifications have been made.

A 1905 view of the one-room schoolhouse on Diamond Rock Hill shows the little building in a state of disrepair. Located on the outskirts of Phoenixville, this small school served children of many ages from the surrounding rural area. The school was originally built in the early 19th century and was first restored in 1909. Today, the building is one of a few surviving one-room schoolhouses in the region and is maintained by a volunteer group.

The Seven Stars Restaurant, located on Route 23, is seen in a photograph from the 1950s. Its consistent quality of service and its landmark status have made the restaurant a favorite among residents and visitors alike. The building, which dates back to 1736, has been operating as a restaurant or an inn for parts of the last few centuries. Although several interior and exterior modifications have been made during the 50 years that separates these images, the restaurant still appears much the same today as it did then.

The Columbia Hotel is seen in this 1949 photograph celebrating Phoenixville's centennial. Signs hanging from the elaborate front porch advertise Schmidt's beer and seafood dinners. To the left of the hotel is the Fraternal Club of the Orioles. Over the years, Phoenixville has been home to many social clubs and fraternal organizations. Today, the Orioles' clubhouse is gone. In its place is the Columbia Hotel parking lot. (Historic image courtesy of the Historical Society of the Phoenixville Area.)

This 1925 photograph shows the Columbia Hotel decorated for Phoenixville's homecoming celebration. This building has been a Phoenixville institution for more than a century. Although it no longer operates as a hotel, it serves the community as a bar and restaurant. The beautiful imported bar is an original and is a one-of-a-kind landmark in its own right. Although the building has been almost entirely redone inside, the exterior maintains many of its original characteristics. (Historic image courtesy of the Historical Society of the Phoenixville Area.)

The F. B. Neiman Funeral Home is located on Gay Street at Morgan Street in this early 20th century photograph. This structure is actually a duplex; the right side was a private residence at the time this photograph was taken. The Neiman Funeral Home later relocated to First Avenue, and this house reverted back to residential use. Today, the homes maintain much of their original exterior character. (Historic image courtesy of the Historical Society of the Phoenixville Area.)

This duplex is located on West Bridge Street at Wheatland Street. The Shewman family is seen standing on the porch of the house on the left. They are celebrating Phoenixville's homecoming festivities in 1910. Many interior and exterior modifications have been made to these homes over the past 95 years, although several original elements remain to this day. The author's family has lived in the former Shewman home for decades. (Historic image courtesy of Joan Benne.)

The original Rhoades family house is seen in a photograph from the late 1920s. This was the farmhouse that sat on the Maple Lawn Farm property, which was located on Route 113 and bordered by Township Line Road. Maple Lawn Farm was developed into a shopping center in the late 20th century. The house is still in use as a private residence. It has undergone several alterations since its original construction. (Historic image courtesy of the Rhoades family.)

Bridge Street merchant David Buck trumpets the latest in modern conveniences in 1910. This was an era when many of Phoenixville's homes lacked indoor plumbing and horse-drawn carriages were a common sight in town. Today, David Buck's original building still stands on Bridge Street at Bank Street, although the front porch supporting this patriotic bunting was removed long ago.

Chapter 2
ADAPTIVE REUSE

The Byrne family residence is seen in 1910. Located at the corner of Second Avenue and Main Street, the building is now home to several offices. The Byrne family was responsible for the construction of St. Ann's Catholic Church, which was made possible by the success of their knitting mill. Except for the removal of the porch roof, the exterior of this structure has retained much of its original charm.

The Byrne knitting mill is seen in this 1904 image. Located on Morgan Street at Lincoln Avenue, the building is still in use today as a business complex. The original photograph shows Morgan Street as a dirt road, while Lincoln Avenue is barely noticeable as a thruway. Although additions were made in the intervening years, some of the same exterior elements of the building are easily recognizable in these two images.

The Church Street School is seen in this 1910 photograph. The school was built in the 1860s and functioned in that capacity for decades before being acquired by the No.1 Fire Company. The upper floors were removed in 1961 and the main floor was converted into the fire company's social hall. The building is located on Church Street near Jackson Street, and the first floor of the original stone structure remains intact.

The Gay Street School is seen in this 1912 photograph. Located on Gay Street at Morgan Street, the building functioned as a school for almost 70 more years after this photograph was taken. It was then converted to an apartment and office complex. Although the façade of the clock tower has changed and part of the grass schoolyard is now a paved lot, much of the building still looks as it did nearly a century ago.

A 1909 photograph shows the Philadelphia and Reading Railroad passenger station, located along the Schuylkill River at the east end of Bridge Street. The ornate spires were removed long ago, but much of the building looks the same today as it did then. Although trains still run along the tracks, they no longer stop at the station. The building now serves the community as a catering hall.

An early 20th century photograph shows a horse-drawn water wagon on Church Street just east of Main Street. The tank is emblazoned with advertisements for a jeweler and a grocer. The stone building in the background was a bank known as the Phoenixville Trust Company, although there was clearly some space allocated to a dentist's office. Although no banking has been done in this building for years, it still functions as commercial space on Main Street. Needless to say, the bars that originally appeared on the windows are no longer necessary.

The Armory Company D building is seen in this 1924 photograph. Despite several changes to the area of Main and Hall Streets over the years—the trolley tracks along Main Street were removed long ago—this building continues to look very much the same. Today, it functions as the Phoenixville Civic Center.

The Phoenixville post office is seen in a 1909 photograph. This building, located on Main Street at Prospect Street, served as the post office for decades until the current post office was constructed on Gay Street. Today, this building remains a viable business and residential structure, although the Main Street façade has been altered on its lower level.

The Thomas A. Evans Box Factory is seen in this 1910 photograph. The building is located on Morgan Street, just west of Lincoln Avenue. Over the years, the original structure has been added onto and has received minor alterations, but it still looks much the same. Several different businesses have occupied the building since box production ceased there many years ago.

The F. W. Woolworth Company five and dime store is seen in this 1912 photograph. Located at the corner of Bridge and Main Streets, this store was a Phoenixville institution for many years. Although the building has lost a couple of stories over the past century, elements of the original structure still remain. The storefronts at this busy intersection still serve a commercial purpose.

The Trio Restaurant was located at 178–180 Bridge Street. Seen here in the late 1960s, the restaurant began operation in the 1940s and enjoyed decades of success before it closed in the 1980s. The only similarities visible in these two photographs are the second- and third-story windows. The first-floor façade and the interior have been dramatically altered since the days of the Trio Restaurant. An interesting detail is the sign hanging on the front of the building, a Cold War relic indicating the presence of a fallout shelter. (Historic image courtesy of Paul Mastrangelo Jr.)

The Trio Restaurant initially occupied only the building at 178 Bridge Street, as seen in this late 1940s photograph. It was originally billed as an Italian restaurant, but its concept evolved over the years. Occupying the space at 180 Bridge Street was the local headquarters of the United Steelworkers of America. This organization supported the employees of Phoenix Steel from this location before moving to a new building across the street prior to the expansion of the Trio. (Historic image courtesy of Paul Mastrangelo Jr.)

The superintendent's building of the Phoenix Iron Company is seen in this 1908 photograph. Located on the east end of Bridge Street, this brownstone building has outlasted almost every other structure that comprised the Phoenix Iron Company, later known as the Phoenix Steel Corporation. The building has been virtually empty and in a state of disrepair for the last several years. As of this writing, it is in the midst of a complete renovation that will adapt it for a new commercial use.

The original Gateway Pharmacy is seen in this 1950s-era photograph. At the outset, the pharmacy was also a popular soda fountain, as evidenced by the advertisement promoting Coca-Cola and Breyer's Ice Cream. The building has received several additions over the years, making the original structure unrecognizable. It still functions as the Gateway Pharmacy and is located on Nutt Road at Gay Street. (Historic image courtesy of the Gateway Pharmacy.)

Chapter 3
A Changing Landscape

The Phoenix Steel property is seen in this 1903 photograph. A vast array of buildings can be seen by the Main Street Bridge over French Creek. At one time, these buildings supported the Phoenix Bridge Company, the Phoenix Iron Company, and, later, the Phoenix Steel Corporation. More than a century later, all of the buildings except for the foundry are gone. The foundry building is the centerpiece of Phoenixville's revitalization efforts and is being adapted for commercial use.

A vast network of railroad tracks appears in an image from 1909. The transportation needs of the Phoenix Steel Corporation were extensive, and transportation was vital to its success. Tons of steel and related products were moved throughout the site daily en route to regional, national, and international destinations. Today, most of the tracks are gone, and it has been decades since a train could be heard rumbling through the site. The only common object in the two photographs is the Main Street Bridge to the right.

This 1986 photograph was taken from the Main Street Bridge, looking west toward the Gay Street Bridge. A forlorn and dilapidated foundry building can be seen on the left side of the image. By the time this photograph was taken, the Phoenix Steel Corporation was in the throes of death. Most of its buildings were unoccupied and awaiting demolition, and the scenery was bleak. Still visible in the current image are elements of the French Creek Dam and an original Phoenix Bridge Company bridge that spanned the narrow waterway.

In this 1940s image, an automotive supply store occupies a storefront that was added to this structure, originally the Hungarian church. Sometime after this photograph was taken, an addition was made to the right side of the structure. The majority of this building, located on Third Avenue at Buttonwood Street, now serves as residential space. The image from early 2005 shows Larry's Barber Shop, a Phoenixville fixture for decades. (Historic image courtesy of the Historical Society of the Phoenixville Area.)

Joshua Rhoades and Buster are seen on Main Street just north of Bridge Street in this early 20th century photograph. To the left, the small wall and steps represent the entrance to the oldest residence in Phoenixville. The two buildings visible on the left are long gone; a municipal parking lot is now in their place. One building that is visible in both images is the grand residence on Vanderslice Street, seen in the distance at the top of both photographs. This building housed the Ukrainian Club for many years and is in the midst of a total restoration at the time of this writing. (Historic image courtesy of the Rhoades family.)

The Detwiler and Dancy Drug Store is seen in this 1912 photograph. Located prominently at the northeast corner of Bridge and Main Streets, this building has been functioning as business space for more than a century. Today, it is occupied by Seacrist's and the Phoenix News Agency. Most of the buildings on the left side of the street still exist, while those on the right were destroyed by fire in the late 1980s. Some of the façades of the remaining buildings have been dramatically altered, and the trolley tracks and horse-drawn wagons are but a distant memory today.

This is a 1905 view of Bridge Street, looking east from the Colonial Theater. To the left is a sign for a restaurant that was located underneath the theater. The first building visible on the left was the original National Bank of Phoenixville. The residence and the large tree at Bank Street are but memories now. Today, the 200 block of Bridge Street represents the heart of the business district and is a hub of commercial activity. Anchored in the center by the historic theater, it is a familiar route for drivers and pedestrians alike.

This view looks west on Bridge Street from Main Street in 1912. Woolworth's and a photography studio are notable structures on the left. This intersection was and still is the center of much activity in Phoenixville. Today, several businesses occupy these structures, although exterior alterations have left most of the façades unrecognizable.

A pre-1910 view of the Colonial Theater shows a building that has changed significantly over the past century. Gone are the vaudeville acts and silent films, but the Colonial continues to operate as a theater and is a gem in the downtown business district. In the historic photograph, a sign directs patrons to the Colonial's restaurant and to a business called Childs. Featured in the Steve McQueen cult-classic movie *The Blob*, the Colonial is still admired by residents and visitors alike.

This is a 1943 photograph of the Colonial Theater, located in the 200 block of Bridge Street near Bank Street. The façade of the theater looks very similar today, although the vertical sign and ticket booth were removed long ago. The ticket booth that once graced the entrance of the theater now sits in a municipal lot in a state of disrepair. To the right is the National Bank of Phoenixville building, which in 1943 was occupied by the Phoenix Recreation Center. Today, it is the home to the *Phoenix*, a local newspaper.

This 1910 photograph was taken from the upper floors of the building that sits on the northwest corner of Bridge and Gay Streets. Looking east on Bridge Street, several businesses are visible, among them Dunlap Grocers, Keinard Brothers, and Klenk Dry Goods. Although the Bridge Street landscape has changed significantly during the years that have elapsed between these two photographs, almost all of the original structures remain intact.

These marchers are heading east on Bridge Street from Gay Street during the centennial parade in 1949. To the left are SunRay drug store, Singer, and McCarraher Brothers Furniture. The Bridge Street landscape has changed significantly over the years. Although many of the businesses are gone, the original structures all remain intact. New commercial enterprises of all sorts now occupy the storefronts beneath changed façades. (Historic image by Viola Batzel.)

A 1925 photograph shows the intersection of Bridge and Gay Streets. The decorations indicate that homecoming week was being celebrated, and even the cars were appropriately adorned. These buildings on Bridge Street are all still intact today, although more than 75 years of renovations have left them looking quite different. The older image shows the now non-existent trolley tracks in the street; back then, there was no need for the traffic lights that we have now.

Part of the 200 block of Bridge Street can be seen in these photographs, taken almost exactly 60 years apart. All of the original structures remain. The astute eye will notice that, at the far left of the older image, a one-way sign directs cars north on Bank Street. This thoroughfare has long since been made a pedestrians-only walkway. Both photographs were taken from in front of the historic Colonial Theater.

The Farmers and Mechanics National Bank can be seen in this 1940s photograph. Built in 1925, the building stands at the corner of Main and Church Streets. Its façade remains largely unchanged. The bank has operated under many names over the years due to various mergers and acquisitions. Visible behind the bank is St. John's Lutheran Church, which was torn down decades ago to make way for the bank's parking lot. A point of interest in this image is the presence of a car traveling westbound on Church Street across Main Street, a one-way street today.

The Farmers and Mechanics National Bank, founded in the late 19th century, can be seen in this 1909 photograph. The original bank building stood at the corner of Main and Church Streets until it was replaced by the present structure in 1925. Through various mergers and acquisitions, it has continued to function as a banking institution for well over 100 years.

Phoenixville Federal Savings is located on Main Street at Hall Street. The building was much smaller when this photograph was taken in 1963 than it is today. The Main Street facility has been expanded dramatically and now features drive-thru lanes and a parking lot that stretches to Church Street. Phoenixville Federal Savings now boasts several branches as well as a multitude of services.

The *c.* 1868 Masonic building can be seen at the left of this 1905 photograph. This view from Church Street looks north on Main Street in the center of town. Although all of the original buildings remain, many alterations have made their façades unrecognizable. A century of progress has also resulted in the destruction of the porches that once hung over the sidewalks on both sides of Main Street.

A view from 1918 shows the Intercounty Bridge spanning the Schuylkill River between Montgomery and Chester Counties. The bridge was built to replace a covered bridge that was destroyed by fire. This bridge served travelers for decades before requiring demolition and replacement. It was blown up in the late 1990s by demolition experts in order to make way for the new bridge. Less ornate and more functional than the original, the new bridge accommodates thousands of travelers each day.

The bridge over the canal on the way to Mont Clare is seen in this early 20th century photograph. The canal system served an important commercial purpose for many years. Today, a variety of recreational opportunities exist at the site. Although the original bridge was replaced long ago, remnants of the stone wall along the right bank still exist. The house in the background was converted to a commercial property many years ago.

The entrance to Reeves Park is located on Main Street between Second and Third Avenues. In this 1911 image, an ornate fountain is visible within a circular fence. Today, the fence remains, but the fountain has been replaced with shrubbery. The park has managed to retain much of its original charm and is still used by residents and civic organizations for a variety of recreational purposes.

This is a 1906 view of Main Street, looking north from Fourth Avenue. At the left is St Ann's Catholic Church. The church looks much the same today as it did when it was built. At the right, a funeral home anchors the block from Fourth Avenue, and a group of residences extends north toward Reeves Park.

An early 20th century photograph shows the Friendship Fire Company on High Street, part of Phoenixville's north side. Although the bell tower is obsolete and has been enclosed, it still remains as part of the structure. The firehouse has maintained some of its original character even as several exterior additions and interior modifications have made it useful and viable in the 21st century.

This 1909 view looks south on the Gay Street Bridge toward downtown Phoenixville. This original bridge had wood planks and elaborate lighting. It was replaced in 1924 by the bridge that currently stands in its place. Known informally as the "high bridge" for its rise over the old Phoenix Steel property, the current bridge is slated to be replaced within the next couple of years.

This church was alternately known as the Hungarian Catholic Church or the Slavish Catholic Church in the early 20th century. It was replaced by Sacred Heart Catholic Church in 1923. The rectory, seen at the right side of both images, is the same building, although it has undergone some minor alterations over the years. The church still commands a strong presence over Phoenixville's skyline from its Church Street location just west of Dean Street.

This 1907 photograph shows the Revolutionary War monument, which marks the farthest point inland reached by the British invasion. The monument sits on a small island of grass at the busy intersection of Bridge Street and Nutt Road. The small fountain pool behind the monument is long gone, but the houses seen under construction in 1907 still exist today.

Washington Field, located on City Line Avenue between Main Street and Gay Street, has been home to Phoenixville High School football for decades. The field is seen in a 1944 photograph showing the original wood grandstand. Today, the field still hosts football and a variety of other sporting events. The only structure that exists in both images is an administration building that was converted from a residence. It is seen on the right side of both photographs. (Historic image courtesy of Albert and Charlotte Lessig.)

Still operating as a farm in the late 1980s, this land was sold and developed at the close of the 20th century. The author's family spent decades farming this plot of land on Pothouse Road just west of Route 29. The farm equipment is gone, although the barn, the 1803 farmhouse, and some outbuildings still exist amongst the new homes. The old driveway has been filled in with grass, and streets have been created on both sides. The oddly shaped tree in the foreground provides some perspective.

This photograph was taken in front of the Phoenix Tavern at Bridge and Gay Streets in 1977. Some of the businesses visible across the street are McCardell's sporting goods store, Troxell's jewelry, Acker and Fry hardware, the State Store, and the Colonial Theater. With the exception of Troxell's and the theater, all of the storefronts and the old tavern are now occupied by other businesses.

A 1988 photograph, taken from East Bridge Street at the base of Church Alley, shows the Columbia Hotel to the left and several buildings that have been marked for demolition. Today, this grassy lot is awaiting development in the 100 block of Bridge Street. The storefront just to the left of the Columbia Hotel was known as Bluejays, a cigar store and social club.

The Hotel Chester is seen in this 1905 view. Over its century-long existence, the building has served in many capacities, including as a hotel, a restaurant, and a bar. In this image, a horse-drawn cart is situated next to the hotel's entrance at what is now the corner of Bridge and Church Streets. The small building to the right was torn down long ago, but the hotel retains much of its original charm and design to this day.

This modest one-story house, seen here in a photograph from 1909, was located on east Bridge Street. The structure was located in the area across from the Columbia Hotel and was part of the Phoenix Steel property. It was demolished long ago for its impracticality and age, and the site is now a parking lot.

Chapter 4
GONE BUT NOT FORGOTTEN

The Dayton Street School, located on Dayton Street just south of Emmett Street on Phoenixville's north side, is seen in this photograph from 1910. This school later operated as the Holy Trinity Catholic Elementary School. It was replaced by a new facility in the 1960s. Today, the Holy Trinity School is no longer in operation as a Catholic school, but it remains part of the Holy Trinity Church complex.

The Phoenixville High School was built in 1911 on Nutt Road near Gay Street. Today, the Phoenixville Hospital occupies the site where the old high school once stood. The school was solid, having been constructed of steel-reinforced concrete, and boasted separate entrances for boys and girls. The building was torn down subsequent to the construction of the new Phoenixville Area High School in 1956.

This house was located on South Main Street at Griffen Street. Although it was originally a residence, it had been used as a doctor's office prior to its demolition in the early 1990s. Today, this site is the southeast corner of Phoenixville Hospital's parking lot. Although many of Phoenixville's grand residences have been preserved, others have been lost to time and progress.

A photograph from the 1940s shows the American Legion Post building on Main Street between Washington Avenue and Morgan Street. The building served the area's veterans as an important central meeting place. In this view, a Breyer's Ice Cream sign hangs beneath a sign for the restaurant located in the lower level of the building. This building was torn down decades ago, and the site is now the parking lot for the Presbyterian Church.

A photograph from 1907 shows the east end of Phoenix Steel near the rear of the superintendent's building on East Bridge Street. The already vast complex was incrementally expanded over the next 70 years. By the 1980s, the lagging economy had brought local steel production to a halt. All that remains at the site today, albeit in a state of disrepair, is the metal pedestrian bridge over French Creek. There is also scant evidence of some foundations, the footprints left behind by an industrial giant.

The shadow of the words "Phoenix Steel Corp." can be seen at the top of this building, which is pictured midway through the demolition process. This 1988 photograph, taken on east Bridge Street, shows the industrial giant in its last days. This scene was captured just behind the brownstone superintendent's building, which still stands on East Bridge Street. All that remains of the complex today are the small pedestrian bridge in the foreground and some remnants of building foundations. As of this writing, the former steel complex is slated for redevelopment.

This photograph from 1883 shows some of Phoenix Steel's buildings, which were eventually torn down in the late 1990s. This photograph was taken from the Shanaman's property on Bridge Street at Taylor Alley. In 2005, all that remains is the original brownstone pump house, the small building visible at the right side of the 1883 image. One of only three remaining buildings of the original Phoenix Steel, the pump house exists in a state of disrepair.

This early 20th century view shows the Battery C building, located on Buchanan Street at Morgan Street. The building sat in front of the armory building, which also faces Buchanan Street. In this historic image, several horses are being paraded through the yard. The armory building was built adjacent to the open garage doors. The Battery C building was torn down in the 1980s, and the armory building now serves a municipal purpose in this borough lot.

The Shanaman Mill and Lumber Company is shown in the 1940s. The west section of the property shown here provided storage for a variety of building materials. This local establishment operated continuously for several decades at its location on Bridge Street at Taylor Alley. After the company ceased operations as a lumber mill, the buildings were retrofitted for use as office space. In 1999, a devastating fire gutted the entire property, and only one portion has been redeveloped as of this writing. The large building to the right contains office space and the new district court.

This view looks west from the Gay Street Bridge in 1990. Clearly visible to the left is the Shanaman Mill and Lumber Company. Shanaman's was destroyed in a 1999 fire, and today a new building, anchored by the district court, sits on the site. To the right, some of Phoenix Steel's many buildings are visible across French Creek. These buildings have been demolished, and the property awaits development.

This photograph from the 1950s shows Jerry's Market, a grocery store on the 300 block of Bridge Street. To the right was Tom's Appliance Store. The Shanaman Mill and Lumber Company is partially visible at the right side of the photograph. Today, the former site of the market is occupied by Phoenix Cleaners, and there is a parking lot to the right. Although many of the storefronts in this part of the business district have stood the test of time, all three of the prominent buildings seen in this historic image have disappeared from the landscape. (Historic image courtesy of the Historical Society of the Phoenixville Area.)

The Johnson-Cowdin Company Silk Mill was located on Franklin Avenue at Grant Street on Phoenixville's north side. This 1909 image shows a large mill building, which was later added to in increments. Over the years, this complex was further developed as the Lachman Carpet Company and later as the Budd Company. As of this writing, the buildings are empty, but the ever-present water tower looms over the community and is the highest structure in town.

The Knoll is seen in this view from 1912. The mansion belonged to Paul Reeves, an executive of the Phoenix Iron Company. The main entrance to the estate was on South Main Street, and fragments of its stone wall still stand in their original place, now the entrance to a housing development. The mansion was torn down decades ago after a period of neglect. Today, the Knollwood apartment complex stands in its place on Nutt Road at the southern end of Starr Street.

This 1908 photograph shows the Phoenixville Hospital, located on Nutt Road between Main Street and Gay Street. This building and subsequent additions stood well into the 1960s, when the current facility was completed. Today, the east end of the Phoenixville Hospital complex occupies the site of the original building.

This grand residence, seen here in 1909, was located on Gay Street at Fourth Avenue. It was torn down in the late 1960s to make way for the Phoenixville Medical Arts Building. The current structure has housed dentists' offices and other businesses over the years.

Phoenixville's centennial parade is captured in this 1949 photograph. Marching east on Church Street from Gay Street, these men are passing by a large house that now represents the site of a municipal parking lot. The house at the left is still there, but it has been converted to apartments. The window pattern on the existing house provides perspective between the two images. (Historic image by Viola Batzel.)

A horse is seen standing in front of the Maple Lawn Auction House in this 1940s photograph. The auction house was but one component of the sprawling Maple Lawn Farm that once graced the intersection of Route 113 and Township Line Road. Auctions were held here for many years, drawing to a close along with the decade of the 1980s. Today, the once-rural setting is home to a composite of shops, fast-food restaurants, a grocery store, and a gas station. (Historic image courtesy of the Rhoades family.)

Richard W. Rhoades is seen sitting atop an ox in the livestock yard at Maple Lawn Farm. The expansive tree in the background represents the approximate site of today's shopping center parking lot, appropriately named Maple Lawn Village. For decades, residents of Phoenixville and nearby towns traveled to Maple Lawn for evening auctions. Farm implements, household goods, antiques, and furniture were sold to the highest bidder. Little remains of this country setting. (Historic image courtesy of the Rhoades family.)

The four-story Phoenix Hotel, seen in this 1912 photograph, stood at the southeast corner of Bridge and Main Streets. The hotel's central location made it one of Phoenixville's most prominent meeting places. To the right, looking up the hill on Main Street, was the All America Shoe Store and the old post office. The building was torn down in 1949, and in its place rose W. T. Grant's, a variety store. Today, the variety store is gone, and the site is now a municipal parking lot.

The General Pike Hotel is seen from the west in this 1994 photograph. Located at the intersection of Routes 113 and 23, the building served for a time as an original stop on the Pony Express mail service route. Operating as a bar in its final days, the structure was torn down shortly after this photograph was taken, despite protests trumpeting its historic value. The old barn to the rear also fell at the same time. More than a decade later, the site still awaits development. The only similarity between these two images is the fast-food establishment to the left in each photograph.

The Phoenix Hose Hook and Ladder Company No. 1 was originally founded in 1874, as indicated on the upper left and right portions of the building. This structure was built in 1900, and the photograph was taken a couple of years later. The current structure, as seen in 2005, was constructed from the remnants of the original firehouse in a 1973–1974 renovation. The firehouse continues to serve the needs of the community from its Church Street location just east of Main Street.